School

And Teacher Student Jokes

R. J. Clarke

School Jokes

How did the dinner lady get an electric shock?
She stepped on a bun and a current went up her leg

Did you hear about the cruel dinner lady?
She beats eggs, batters fish and whips cream

Why did the book need to be sent to hospital?
Because it's got a broken spine

Did you hear about the kidnapping at school?
He eventually woke up

Why do magicians do so well at school?
Because they are good at trick questions

Why did the amoeba do so bad at math?
Because it multiplied by dividing

What shape was in a car crash?
A wrecked angle

How did you find school today?
I just got off the bus and there it was

What did the inflatable teacher at an inflatable school say to the inflatable child holding a pin?
You let me down, you let your school down but most of all… you let yourself down

Why did the schoolboy take a ladder to school?
Because he thought it was a high school

What is a physics teacher's favorite meal?
Fission chips

Why did the teacher go cross-eyed?
Because she couldn't control her pupils

What do you call a teacher who doesn't fart in public?
A private tooter

What type of school did surfers go to?
Boarding school

What happened when the teacher tied all of the students shoe laces together?
They had a class trip

Why did the students eat their homework?
Because their teacher said it was a piece of cake

What do you call a teapot that is placed on the top shelf and left to boil water?
High-pot-in-use

What happened to the plant when it was moved in to the mathematics class?
It grew square roots

Why was the student's report card so wet?
His grades were below C-Level

Why did a girl write an essay whilst sitting on a horse?
Because her teacher told her to write an essay on her favorite animal

Why don't farts graduate from high school?
Because they always get expelled

What did the computer say to a keyboard?
You're not my type

Why did the Cyclops give up teaching?
Because he only had one pupil

How do bees get to school?
They use the school buzz

What would happen if you took the school bus home?
The police would make you return it

Why did the neutron get a free drink?
Because there was no charge

What are you going to be when you leave school?
An old man

Why do math teachers care about every one of their students?
Because every student counts

Why are fish so clever?
Because they swim in schools

Why did the students solve their math problems on the floor?
Because the teacher told them not to use tables

Why did the ground laugh at the earthquake?
Because the ground was starting to crack up

What did the glue stick say to the other glue stick?
We have to stick together

What do snakes like to study?
Hissstory

Why did the musician do so well at school?
She took lots of notes

Why was the schoolgirl too hot?
She was wearing a blazer

Why did the teacher wear sunglasses?
Because she had the brightest class in the school

Who is the king of your desk?
Your ruler

What is a computers favorite animal?
A mouse

Why did the sun never go to university?
Because it has 15 million degrees

How did the Dark Ages get its name?
From the knights

When do astronauts eat?
At launch time

How did the music teacher get out of a locked classroom?
She realized her keys were on the piano

What did the ghost teacher say to his pupils?
Look at the board and I'll go through it again

What subject has the most fruits in it?
History because it has so many dates

Why did the student throw a clock out of the window?
He wanted to see time fly

What letter can hurt you?
Bee

Who is a penguins favorite aunt?
Aunt Arctica

What happens if you throw your school books in the ocean?
You get a title wave

What is the dullest chemical element on the periodic table?
Bohrium

What grades did sailors get when they were at school?
High C's

Why did the silly boy eat some coins?
Because his mother told him it was his lunch money

Why did the student think that the teacher loved him?
There was lots of X's on his homework

What is a pirate's favorite subject?
Arrrrrt

How are computers like hallways?
They both have monitors

What did Sherlock Holmes investigate when he was a schoolboy?
A pencil case

Why are chemistry teachers good at solving problem?
Because they have all of the solutions

What type of school did King Arthur go to?
Knight school

What is a cow's favorite subject?
Moo-sic

What career does a spider have?
A web designer

Where do you go to learn how to make icecream?
Sundae school

Where do pencils come from?
Pennsylvania

Why is Alabama the smartest state in the USA?
Because it has four A's and one B

Why did the bird go to the library?
To find some bookworms

What does a nose and feet have in common?
A nose runs and feet can smell

I was going to tell you a joke about sodium...
But Na

Why did the student crawl into class?
Because the teacher told him not to walk in late

Why did the student wear glasses in her mathematics class?
Because it improves di-vision

Why did the little boy get punished for something he didn't do?
Because he didn't do his homework

What did the map say to the other map?
Atlas, we're together

What did the math book say to the other math book?
Stop bothering me, I have my own problems

When is a blue exercise book not blue?
When it is read

What is a geologist teacher's favorite type of music?
Rock music

Why did the spider wear glasses?
To improve its website

How did the Vikings send secret messages?
Norse code

Where is the best place to grow flowers?
In Kindergarden

Why did the student bring scissors to his class?
Because he wanted to cut class

Why did the students stop going to the library?
Because they heard it was fully booked

What tools should you bring to math class?
Multi-pliers

Why was the music teacher so good at baseball?
Because she had the perfect pitch

Why did the teacher go to the beach?
To test the water

What does a computer do at the beach?
It surfs the net

Which building has the most stories?
The library

Why did the clock go to the principal's office?
Because it was tocking too much

How did the cyber bully get out of prison?
He found the escape key

What is a moth's favorite subject?
Mothematics

Why did the computer go to the doctors?
Because it had a virus

Which king invented fractions?
Henry the 1/8th

Why did the nose not want to go school?
It was tired of being picked on

Why did the student study in an airplane?
To get a higher education

What is a librarians favorite vegetable?
Quiet peas

What does a mermaid wear?
An algae-bra

Why did the jellybean go to school?
It wanted to be a Smartie

Why did the student think that the chemical formula for water was: H I J K L M N O?
Because his teacher told him it was H to O

What's the difference between a teacher and a train?
A teacher says, "Spit out that gum" whilst a train says, "Choo, choo"

Why did the art teacher take a pencil to bed?
So that she could draw the curtains

What did the sharpner say to the pencil?
Can you stop going around in circles and get to the point

Why did the girl sleep in class?
She wanted to follow her dreams

What country is really spicy?
Chile

What type of ship do smart kids travel on?
A scholar-ship

What was the biologist teacher wearing to class?
Designer jeans

How do you get straight A's?
Use a ruler

Why couldn't the schoolboy go straight home after school?
Because he lived around the corner

Why did the echo get detention?
Because it answered back

What did the calculator say to the other calculator?
You can count on me

Where do books sleep?
Under their covers

What is the difference between cats and commas?
Cats have claws at the end of paws, whilst a comma is a pause at the end of a clause

Why was the spit ball gun confiscated?
Because it was a weapon of math disruption

What did the gossip queen say when she heard about Oxygen and Magnesium getting together?
OMg

Why did the teacher write on the window?
She wanted to make her lesson clear

Why was a schoolkid locked in a cage?
He was the teacher's pet

Where was the declaration of Independence signed?
At the bottom

What do you call the small rivers that flow into the River Nile?
Juveniles

Who was the fattest knight at King Arthur's round table?
Sir Cumference. His large size was because of the Pi

Why was the obtuse angle beginning to boil?
Because it was over 90 degrees

What do you call a small angle?
A-cute angle

What did the physics teacher say to the crying child?
Watts up?

Why do chemistry teachers like nitrates?
Because they are cheaper than day rates

What did the volcano say to the other volcano?
I lava you

What type of tree do math teachers climb?
Geometry

What shape can be used to catch any animal?
A trapezoid

Why was the computer tired?
Because it had a hard drive

What do you call a number that can't sit still?
A roamin' numeral

What type of music do balloons hate?
Pop

What do you call a nervous javelin thrower?
Shakespeare

How did the music teacher teach math?
With an algorithm

What did the pencil say to the other pencil?
You're looking sharp

Why can't you do an exam in the savanna grasslands?
Because there are too many cheetahs

Why aren't cowboys allowed in art class?
Because when they are asked to draw, they fire their guns

What's worse than finding a caterpillar in your salad?
Finding half a caterpillar

Why was the cafeteria clock slow?
It went back four seconds

Why did a student take a bat into the library?
Because his teacher told him that he needed to hit the books

How does a tree go on the internet?
It logs on

What do you call a professional tractor driver?
A protractor

Why did the student think she needed a new teacher?
Because the teacher was always asking her for the answers

What did the square say to the circle?
I haven't seen you round here before

What happens when a chemistry joke is not funny?
There's no reaction

How did Ben Franklin feel when he discovered that thunderstorms are made from electricity?
He was shocked

Which tower in France cannot eat anything?
The Eifel (I full) tower

When does a computer need new shoes?
When it is rebooting

What did the frog say at the library?
Read it, read it

Where can you buy a 3 foot ruler?
At a yard sale

What does a mathematician do if he gets wax in his ears?
He works it out with a pencil

What do you do with a sick chemistry teacher?
First you try Helium, then Curium and if all that fails, your only option is Barium

Why was the computer cold?
Because it forgot to close its windows

Why did the teacher marry the janitor?
Because she was swept off her feet

What is the longest piece of furniture in the classroom?
The multiplication table

What is the longest word?
Smiles because there is a mile between each S

What do you call a person reading a book about the mind?
A mind reader

What do you call a naughty boy in music class?
In treble

What happens when you read a book about anti-gravity?
You can't put it down

What do story tellers and dogs have in common?
They both have tails

What did the hungry boy get on his IQ test?
Saliva

What did the earthquake say when he was accused of causing the ground to open up?
It's not my fault

Why did the mushroom go to the party?
Because he's a fun guy

What travels faster, heat or cold?
Heat because you can catch a cold

Who solves electrical mysteries?
Sherlock Ohms

How do you prevent diseases caused by biting insects?
Don't bite any

Teacher Student Jokes

Teacher: You missed school didn't you?
Student: Not really

Teacher: How can you make so many mistakes in one day?
Student: I get up early

Teacher: You look like you need to go to the toilet. I'll let you go but I'd like to hear you say the alphabet first
Student: ABCDEFGHIJKLMNOQRSTUVWXYZ
Teacher: Very good but where's the P?
Student: Dribbling down my leg

Teacher: Did your father help you with your homework?
Student: No, he did it all by himself

Teacher: If I had 9 oranges in one hand and 9 oranges in another hand, what would I have?
Student: Big hands

Teacher: Who led the children of Israel across the Red Sea?
Student: It wasn't me miss, honest

Teacher: The first kid to answer my question can go home early

A student throws his bag out of the window

Teacher: Who threw that?

Student: Me, I'm going home now

Teacher: I want the class to answer my question at once. What is 5+8?

Students: At once

Teacher: Could you please pay a little attention?

Student: I am paying as little attention as I can

Teacher: Can you name two days that start with the letter T?

Student: Today and Tomorrow

Teacher: How can you prove that the Earth is round?

Student: I can't. Besides, I never said it was

Teacher: Where is your homework?

Student: I lost it during a fight with a kid that said you weren't the best teacher in the whole school

Teacher: What are you going to write your essay on?

Student: Paper

Teacher: What chemical does HCl stand for?
Student: Oh, oh, I got it on the tip of my tongue
Teacher: You had better spit it out because it's hydrochloric acid

Teacher: Say a sentence that begins with the letter I?
Student: I is the…
Teacher: I'm going to have to stop you there because you should never put the word is after I. What you need to use is the word am
Student: Ok. I am the ninth letter of the alphabet

Teacher: Stand up if you're an idiot
A student stood up
Teacher: Are you an idiot?
Student: No miss, I just felt bad that you were the only one standing up

Teacher: I hope I didn't see you looking at someone else's exam paper
Student: I hope you didn't either

Teacher: Do you like doing homework?
Student: I like nothing better

Teacher: Why are you late?
Student: Because a sign said, "School Ahead, Go Slow"

37565751R00015

Printed in Great Britain
by Amazon